THE SPORTO

Tales from the Rock Mecca of South Florida

The Hollywood Sportatorium

A First-Hand Account of the 1980's Hard Rock Scene

Dedicated to the 1980's Hard Rock Bands and the Fans that followed them.

Something's at the edge of your mind
You don't know what it is
Something you were hoping to find
But you're not sure what it is
Then you hear the music
And it all comes crystal clear
The music does the talking
Says the things you want to hear

TRIUMPH

Special Dedication to the Hard Rock Bands

Quiet Riot, Poison, Ratt, Bon Jovi, Skid Row, Mötley Crüe, Twisted Sister, Warrant, Slaughter, WASP, White Lion, Firehouse, Tesla, Queensrÿche, Dokken, Stryper, Night Ranger, Val Halen, Iron Maiden, Triumph, Great White and more...

Extra Dedication to Fleetwood Mac

THE SPORTO

COPYRIGHT © 2015 BY C. RICH

All rights reserved. Printed in the United States of America. No part of this book may be used or reproduced in any manner whatsoever without written permission except in the case of brief quotations embodied in critical articles or reviews.

I have tried to recreate events, locales and conversations from my memories of them. In order to maintain their anonymity in some instances I have changed the names of individuals and places, I may have changed some identifying characteristics and details such as physical properties, occupations and places of residence.

Book & Cover design by Twin Rivers

Communications

Editor R. A. Biest
Photos by Mark Marovitch

ISBN: 978-1517162368

First Edition: September 2015
Second Edition: July 2025

10 9 8 7 6 5 4 3 2 1

Other Works by C. Rich

The Misers of Miramar
Theory of the Infinite Mind
Poli-sci-smic
UnPresidented Trump
The Golden Escalator
Amazing Saga of Mamaluke
Down the Road to Operation Senior Sentinel
Lost in a Maze of Discontent
Up the River Paddle Not Included
Baby Boomers Destroyed the World
Club Suicide
Bloody Newsroom
The Relationship Reconstruction Project
Ten Days of Craigslist
The Casey Anthony Trial

Prologue

Billy Joel once called it "an acoustic nightmare." Rodger Waters called the place "a real compromise." And Robert Plant said, "This is the first gig I've ever done that was rained out *inside the building*." However, what they might not have understood at the time was that this place was a temple to all of us in South Florida. It was a sacred place where we would gather and worship at the altar of Hard Rock. It was where we went to hear angels sing. It was the place the rock god Brian Johnson screamed out, "Oh, Let there be rock!" I am talking about the Hollywood Sportatorium in the 1980s. I'm talking about a place in Rock 'n' Roll history that existed for 18 years as the only venue of its kind in all of South Florida to see rock music live.

The Hollywood Sportatorium, or The Sporto as we called it, was the venue in South Florida where everyone came to play like Bon Jovi, Cinderella, Def Leppard, Guns N' Roses, Iron Maiden, Judas Priest, Mötley Crüe, Night Ranger, Poison, Quiet Riot, Ratt, Triumph, Foreigner, Twisted Sister and Van Halen just to name a handful. It was the place where we would all go to see all of our favorite bands. If you were a rock band and you never played the Sporto, then you just hadn't made it to the top like Foreigner sang about in the song "Jukebox Hero." The Sporto was an arena that held 15,532 rock souls and was *THE* place for live rock concerts in South Florida.

The building does not exist anymore. However, it still stands in the four corners of my heart and soul. I can still see the whole place in my mind's eye. I can still smell the cigarette and pot smoke in the air. If I close my eyes long enough, I can hear the sounds of the last Heavy Metal Band to ever play there, Judas Priest in September of 1988 singing "Turbo Lover." Some of the best memories of my entire life lie forever in the four walls of the Hollywood Sportatorium. I heard some of the greatest bands the world of music had to offer. I heard bands right in the middle of their prime. I saw bands play before anyone knew who they were, and I watched bands play long after their peak and everything in between. I stood witness to the greatest era in rock 'n' roll. I stood in abject awe watching and listening to the last generation of master musicians that could actually play their instruments. I came of age in a magical time in music. I was there and grew up during 1980's Hard Rock Scene.

Chapter One: The 80s

Anyone who has ever said anything negative about the 1980s and the rock bands that sprung up during that decade does not know what they're talking about. I have heard in my lifetime people use the term "Hair Bands" in an effort to talk down this era in rock 'n' roll music. They say it as if all of that long hair back then was everything that genre had to offer. That it was more about the fashion and not the music. Somehow a dismissive attitude was attributed and developed around this time in rock history. I'm not sure how that all started, but anyone who believes this misnomer is missing out on a great era in music as far as I am concerned. I know rock fans circle around the 1960s or the 1970s as the greatest decades in rock music. I love both of those decades as well, but if I were to be dropped on a desert island for all of time and could only choose one decade of rock music, the 80s would be my choice hands down. By the time this decade of rock music came around the musicians of this era fine-tuned the art of playing their instruments to a master level. No one before or after them took to elevating certain instruments like the guys in the Hard Rock Bands did. By the time the 80s came around Eddie Van Halen of Van Halen was doing things with a guitar never seen before or after in all of music. Neil Peart of Rush was hitting his peak with drums, and nobody could or would reach that skill level with a drum set ever again. Steve Harris of Iron Maiden was literally reinventing the bass guitar, while David Lee Roth and Vince Neil redefined what being a front man really meant. With all of that, and some of the best songs written by a bunch of the greatest song writers and poets of all time, then you can see why the 1980s Hard Rock era reigns king.

I grew up in South Florida in the 1970s and came of age in the 1980s. It was my generation that bore witness to the birth of MTV. Cable Television was taking off and this became our favorite channel in our basic cable package. Back when MTV actually played music 24/7, we were able to see live performances of Hard Rock bands on our television sets. During this time, we carved out what I now called *Hair Nation* and built a community around a show on MTV called *Head Bangers Ball*. Here we would see live performance videos of our favorite rock bands and then wait for the bands to tour and come through our town to play. In South Florida, back then, there was only one place big enough for these bands to play. Every band of note at the time played the Hollywood Sportatorium or the Sporto as we called it. The building looked like an airplane hangar and was built of concrete with a steel roof. It was built by the man who brought South Florida some of the greatest venues such as Calder Race Track and Miami-Hollywood Motorsports Park. The Sporto was built with the idea of bringing some kind of sports franchise to South Florida. Over the years the effort to attract a major sports team to our arena failed, while not so quietly, the Sporto was turning into a legendary house of rock where every major musical act would come and play.

The arena was built on the outskirts of all the cities off a two-lane road in a town called Pembroke Pines. The Sporto was in the western end of Broward County, Florida towards the Everglades. This area of South Florida was not developed at the time and because of the two-lane road the traffic problems getting to and from the arena became legendary. Cars would overheat in bumper-to-bumper traffic and people would just leave their automobiles behind and walk to the Sporto. Some of those people who left their cars in the road were then run over by other cars and killed by other people who were also trying to get to the arena. There was not a whole lot that would keep any of us from seeing our favorite bands including dead bodies, bad weather or the Broward County Sheriff's Office. I personally left my girlfriend behind on the cement steps of the Sporto swimming in a puddle of her own vomit as soon as I heard Sammy Hagar play his first notes. Don't get me wrong, she was a cool chick, but I was 16 years old, and this was Van Halen's first tour with Sammy Hagar. I wasn't going to miss it because she couldn't handle her booze. She would have to fend for herself. I'd have to find her later.

The Sporto patrons were a rough crowd, to say the least. If a band started late, they would start a riot. If the Sportatorium was late opening the gates, they would scale the eleven-foot wall. If the cops bothered them, they would attack the cops with rocks and glass bottles and fight them fist to fist. The music fans even held thirty-five cops hostage in a trailer for over an hour when they took some of their friends to their command center over some marijuana. When Bruce Springsteen complained on stage about them throwing firecrackers at him, people just jumped on stage to put out the smoking fireworks by pissing all over it. After a while the cops would just tear gas everyone when they got too rowdy. It was an amazing time and place. There was nothing like it. At times it was completely out of control. But then there were times when the collective buzz would peak, and the music would hit just the right vibe bringing us to Music Utopia. At that very moment we understood perfection and being alive. We were connected to the music. The music was our heartbeat. It was like a spiritual awakening and it happened a lot in that building which made the Sporto so special. It felt like magic and I will never forget it as long as I live.

With all that being said, I lived in that place. I grew up in that arena. I was a typical Broward guy who knew how lucky we were to have such an arena in our county. My friend Chuck and I tried to see every concert that came through that was Hard Rock or so-called Glam Metal. The Glam Metal scene came out of Los Angeles in the 1980s and spread out across the country. It was a time when men put on makeup and all the guys pieced their ears. A certain sound in music came about that was later tagged "Hair Band," but for me it was just Hard Rock with a flare. It was my kind of music.

I want you, the reader, to go grab a glass of wine, a cocktail or maybe a puff of some good smoke. I want you to kick up your feet and sit back and read about the Hollywood Sportatorium in the 1980s. I want to tell you about the bands we fell in love with and followed long after the Sporto was gone. Let me tell you some stories about the Rock Mecca of South Florida through the blazed eyes and memory of someone who was actually there. This was the

Sporto, the bands and me. These are just a few more tales told from The Last Generation of Freedom.

Chapter Two: 1977

Admittedly the Sporto was something that meant more to my family than most others. My mother took me to see my first live concert there at the age of eleven on August 6, 1980 to see Fleetwood Mac. I personally have seen so many bands there that I forget some of them. My father actually worked security at the Sporto when Elvis kicked off his last tour in 1977 just months before he died. Even my dog knew the Hollywood Sportatorium because my dad took him and a billy club to work security at that Elvis concert. So everybody in my house including the family dog had a relationship with the Sporto at one time or another.

I was seven years old when my family migrated from New York City to Miramar, Florida. That first year when my father got that gig to work security at the Sporto was a night I remember clearly because my mother was so full of joy that my dad took that job. My parents loved Elvis. My family was unaware of the reputation of the Sporto but knew any Elvis concert could get out of hand. I remember my father putting on his leather jacket to go. I helped him put the muzzle on our family dog who was a Belgium Sheepdog. I don't know if you have ever seen this kind of dog, but they look just like a black wolf. Our dog was named Sergeant and I helped my father put on the steel muzzle around his mouth and strapped it to his head. My father opened the closet door in the hallway of our house and pulled out a wooden octagon-shaped billy club that had a rope on the end of it. Pop wrapped the rope around his hand, grabbed the dog leash I had already put on our dog and walked out the front door with my mother. I stood in the doorway waving as my father, mother and dog got in the family car and drove away.

That night my babysitter and I sat on the couch under the front window of our home and she played Elvis records all night. My parents were big music fans and they loved Elvis, so we had plenty of albums to choose from. As the night went on, we fell asleep on the couch with the stereo making that sound the record player makes when the needle is just stuck at the end of a song while the record spins on the turntable: click, click, click.

In the early morning hours we were awoken by my father, mother and our dog returning from the Sporto. We sat up on the couch and asked Pop how it went. He was beaming from head to toe and said Elvis was incredible. He said the crowd and the arena were so wild that they had to land a helicopter at the Sportatorium to create a diversion while they snuck Elvis in on a Greyhound Bus. He said Elvis told the crowd, "You sure look like a great audience, Ladies and Gentlemen," and the crowd started to surge towards the stage. Dad said people were forced out of their seats and some left the arena all angry because of it. He said people were screaming and light bulbs were going off like mad from the cameras.

Apparently, some people were demanding their money back because they lost their seats or their view got blocked by the crowd. Dad said the cops were trying to get the people in wheelchairs out of the arena for their own safety. He said Elvis threw autographed scarves into the crowd and people got hurt fighting over them. He said the crowd just kept trying to get closer and closer to the stage, but the show went on. He said it was a great show and for the most part he said people loved it. Mom was just happy because she got to go backstage.

Six months later on August 16, 1977, my parents completely fell apart when the news hit that Elvis had died. My father held my mother in his arms for hours sitting on the couch in front of the TV as they both cried endlessly. I'll never forget that day. That was the first time I saw my father cry. My family had this connection to Elvis and because of the Sportatorium it became very personal to our household. To this day, whenever you see pictures of the bloated Elvis right before he died, many of those pictures came from that night at the Hollywood Sportatorium. The Sporto was a part of history and it became part of our family as well.

Chapter Three: 1980

Fast forward nearly three years and that loving couple cuddling on the couch over the death of Elvis is now divorced. My father moved away to Ocala, FL. My mother was now a single mom in the 1980s with three kids and working three jobs. I became an eleven-year-old kid with a paper route trying to bring in some money and begging my mother to take me to my first concert.

I finally got my mom and a few of her lady friends to take me to my first live show. It was decided that I would go to see Fleetwood Mac on August 6, 1980 playing at the Hollywood Sportatorium. Fleetwood Mac was on the third leg of their North American part of their world tour that went across the globe. By the time the band made it to the Sporto there was less than a month left to go on this tour that nearly ripped the band apart.

Unbeknownst to any of us, Fleetwood Mac was in big trouble as a band at that time and they were on the verge of breaking up.

The group was on their *Tusk* Tour promoting that album and the tour itself became a case study in indulgent spending and debauchery. The band was tearing itself apart. The whole band was playing out every rock and roll cliché in the book. Because they were blowing all the money the tour was making, the decision was made to tape all the live shows, to make a live album and try to recoup some of the lost money due to excesses like private jets and unlimited cocaine. While the band was abusing each other mentally and physically, they were about to play for me at my very first live concert.

I wonder if any band truly understands how their music touches people. I wonder if they get so lost in themselves sometimes and forget us, the fans. At the very same time Fleetwood Mac was devolving, I was an eleven-year-old kid who was about to go to my first live show. I was about to be touched by the experience forever. I prepared for the concert like any other kid would. I locked myself in my bedroom for weeks on end listening to my albums trying to learn all their songs. I had both the *Rumours* and *Tusk* albums and I listened to them over and over again getting ready for the night. I knew nothing of the band's troubles. I just fell in love with their music in my bedroom and was about to be exposed to live music for the first time.

The night came and I got in the car with my mom and a few of her friends. It was my first experience with the infamous traffic problems getting out to the Sporto. The ride became a party in itself when the bumper-to-bumper traffic hit. The ladies in the car pulled out some joints and started to smoke weed while blaring Fleetwood Mac from the car speakers. A quick glance at the cars and the people around us revealed to me everyone was on the same magic carpet ride. It was a different time and place back then when my mom's friends passed me the joint and I too partook in the forbidden pleasure of that magical plant.

When we got to the Sporto I just looked up in wonderment and awe at this nondescript type building. It looked like an airplane hangar. We walked inside and found our seats, which were on the right side of the stage if you were in the building looking straight forward. They were pretty damn good seats I found out years later. Inside, the excitement of the night was in the air, along with all of the cigarette and pot smoke. The room had an incredible vibe to it.

When the lights went down and the music filled the darkness everyone started to scream with excitement. That excitement spread through the arena from person to person and created a collective joy that pulsed through my body. I was never the same again. Live music held some kind of magical hold over me. I never felt anything like it. It has never faded to this day and it all started that night in the Sporto with Fleetwood Mac. My taste in music had a sharper turn towards Hard Rock, but I will never forget how great Fleetwood Mac sounded live that night. I'll never forget how beautiful Stevie Nicks looked in person. I think people forget how absolutely stunning she really was back then. Something happened to me and I was never the same again after that night. Live music affected me in a completely different way than studio music. Don't get me wrong, I love a well-tailored or sculpted album of perfection, but that raw sound of live music has no equal. This was the beginning for me. I love the way the imperfection of playing live music dances around the perfect studio version of a song. I was enamored with the fact that songs played live never seem to sound the same way twice. That night live music and that building became a big part of my life. That was my first concert. It was an undeniable part of my upbringing and I could not think of a better way to come of age. This is my story and I am guessing I am not the only one.

Chapter Four: 1982

Growing up in Miramar, Florida, I was exposed to all sorts of music. I feel I got a little taste of almost everything to listen to back then. Pop music was big with the ladies and the guys liked everything from country to Heavy Metal. The punk music scene was pretty strong in South Florida with all of the skateboarders and surfers. I even learned Motown from my mom and The Rolling Stones from my dad. I was exposed to The King of Country, Johnny Cash, by my stepfather and even one of my friends was a Beatles fan. With all of those musical influences that surrounded me at the time no other genre touched my soul like Hard Rock. The hard music spoke to my very inner self. As far back as I remember I was collecting KISS cards and not baseball cards like other kids. I endured all of the unsophisticated rumors about Devil music and all of the finger pointing over guys with long hair. Nothing, and I mean nothing would sway me away from Hard Rock. The music was just too superior over the lighter stuff. The level at which the musicians of Hard Rock took their instruments was something I could not turn my head to and ignore. These guys were the modern-day Beethoven or Bach as far as I was concerned.

In 1979 and 1980 two albums were released that would change my life forever and cement my taste in music. In February of 1979 *Cheap Trick at Budokan* was released in America and the sound of that live album reverberated through my body. Listening to the thousands of screaming Japanese all I wanted to do was be there in the crowd with them. Born in 1969 I was at the perfect age to hear the message, "Your mommy's all right, your daddy's all right, they just seem a little weird surrender, surrender, but don't give yourself away," and not only understand it, but feel it in my bones.

The second album that touched my soul was released in the U.S. in July of 1980 by an Austrian band called AC/DC. The name of the album was *Back in Black*. From beginning to end, that album became the soundtrack to my life. The guitarist Angus Young was the first musician that made me understand that there is another level to playing one's instruments. To this day, all I have to hear is just one chord and I know it is him playing. Angus taught me that a person could have a signature sound and speak through the guitar in such a way that it becomes its own language. The hard sound of that band, exposed to me at that perfect age, created a Hard Rock fan that would last my whole life.

By the time the 1980s came around the world of Hard Rock was in transition. Led Zeppelin's drummer John Bonham was dead and the group disbanded. The lead singer of AC/DC, Bon Scott, died and was replaced by Brian Johnson. A woman named Pat Benatar was rocking out arenas and Ozzy Osbourne teamed up with Randy Rhoads to make music history with the *Blizzard of Ozz* album. An incredible decade of Hard Rock was taking hold. Sadly, when most people look back on the 1980s they highlight what was going on in Pop music and ignore the Hard Rock scene altogether.

It was now 1982 and I was old enough to go to the Hollywood Sportatorium by myself or with my friends. This was the year I would pick the bands I would go see live. Bless my mom and Fleetwood Mac, but it was time to go see a Hard Rock show. The year started off with Ozzy biting off the head of a bat and landing up in the hospital while also getting arrested for urinating all over The Alamo in Texas. So much was going on that year. Hard Rock fans lost a kindred when Randy Rhodes died in Florida in a freak plane accident. Iron Maiden got a new singer, Bruce Dickinson, and put out their greatest album of all times. At the same time Christians across America started burning that Iron Maiden album and Ozzy's albums in protest to what they called satanic music. It was a great time to be a Hard Rock fan. Many acts came to the Sporto in 1982 like AC/DC, Black Sabbath without Ronnie James Dio and Heart. I chose as a neophyte concert goer Van Halen to be my very first live show that year. Van Halen was at their peak on their *Hide Your Sheep*

Tour and was supporting one of the best albums they ever made called *Diver Down*. David Lee Roth and the Boys, as history shows, were literally at their peak musically. The band was on fire that year. It was the perfect live show for me at the time to go see.

In South Florida in the 1980s if you wanted to go to a concert at the Sporto and did not have a credit card, you had to go to the Hollywood Mall off of Park Road to a music store that had a Ticketmaster's machine in it. Since none of the kids in my neighborhood had credit cards, we would either have to ride our bikes to the Hollywood Mall or take a city bus to it from Miramar. The Hollywood Mall became famous nationally a year earlier when Adam Walsh was kidnapped and his father John Walsh became a crime activist. *America's Most Wanted* TV show sprung out from that mall in the 1980s. Mothers and fathers held on to their children's hands a lot tighter after all of that when walking around that mall and other malls. I remember the kidnapping like it was yesterday.

Getting the tickets to the Van Halen concert was easy the first time because I told an older girl who lived on my block that I was going to go. She was old enough to have her own car and offered me a ride to the mall if I would go to see Van Halen with her. She was a girl that is sometimes referred to as a "Butter Face" which meant everything was sexy, but her face. She had a body that would stop a clock but her face was not easy on the eyes. I took her up on her offer and on December 9, 1982 I went to the Sporto to see Van Halen live. We smoked pot in the car the entire way there. When we finally parked at the arena she offered me my very first blowjob. A man never forgets that first one and in the parking lot of the Sporto sitting in a gold colored 1976 Plymouth Duster, Butter Face went down on me. It was a great way to start off the night.

Van Halen was magical that night. David Lee Roth ran around the stage like a mad man possessed. He was the ultimate front man. Eddie Van Halen did a guitar solo that was to die for. The band sang some of my favorite songs like "Unchained," "Ice Cream Man" and "Everybody

Wants Some." The Sporto was packed and they sold out and did another concert the next day. I feel so lucky that I saw Van Halen play in 1982. It really was special. They are old guys now and can't do that stuff anymore but I knew them when they could.

Chapter Five: 1983

By the time 1983 came around the Hard Rock scene was in full force. The year started off with Def Leppard releasing their third album called *Pyromania* and Hard Rock was off and running. Songs like "Rock of Ages" and "Photograph" filled the airways. Quiet Riot exploded on the scene with their number one album called *Metal Health* and knocked Michael Jackson's album *Thriller* out of the number one spot selling a million albums a week. The Glam Metal scene skyrocketed out of Los Angeles and spread across the nation influencing a new band out of Texas called Pantera. They called it Glam Metal at the time, but later Pantera would be classified Speed Metal. It was all semantics, because to me, it was all different levels of Hard Rock. That year a band called Metallica debuted their very first album called *Kill 'Em All* and started a whole movement of rock fans who liked their Speed Metal. Meanwhile I was gravitating more towards a traditional form of Glam Metal out of Los Angeles with bands like Motley Crüe, Quiet Riot and Ratt. One of the benefits about the Glam Metal Scene was the fact that tons of ladies got into that kind of music. If you went to a Pantera or Metallica concert for an example, the crowd was mostly dudes. It felt like you were standing in the middle of a sausage factory. The Glam Metal concerts were loaded with female fans and being a young, red-blooded American, it wasn't much of a choice for me. I went with the Glam scene. It did not hurt that the music was great as well.

In South Florida guys around this time started to pierce their ears. Actually, to be more accurate we pierced one ear. When men started to pierce their ears there was this social connotation that if you pierced only your left ear then you were straight. If you pierced the right ear or both, that meant you were gay. I don't know how that started, but that was in fact how it was for a while in the beginning. That social axiom finally did go away, but it was serious business back then. One would have to be very careful about the piercing of the ears so as not to bring violence and bigotry down on oneself. When I finally decided to pierce my left ear my stepsister helped me do it with a needle and an ice cube. It was a bloody mess, but it worked. My mother came home from work that day and saw my ear pierced and sat at our dining room table and cried for a long time. She thought her son was being influenced by evil forces. Little did I know at the time, but when I would listen to my music in my bedroom, my Irish Catholic mother would be on the other side of the wall in her bedroom with a framed picture of me placed on her dresser as she knelt down in front of it, praying to God to save my soul. She thought I was listening and caught up by the devil and the so-called devil music. When she saw me grow my hair longer and pierce my ear, she lost it completely thinking Satan was making me gay. The next day I sent roses to her job and we never talked about it again. Looking back at it all, clearly it was another time and place and I should feel lucky she did not bring in a Catholic priest to do an exorcism. We were paving our own paths as head bangers. We were very misunderstood.

In 1983 all of the hot new bands came to the Hollywood Sportatorium. That year KISS, Pat Benatar, and Def Leppard came though and played the Sporto. Iron Maiden, Quiet Riot and Loverboy also came through and rocked out South Florida, but my favorite concert that year hands down was Ratt. This was the year Ratt exploded onto the music scene and released their first self-entitled album. They were so raw and amazing at the time. MTV was giving them heavy rotation on television playing songs like "Round and Round" or "Wanted Man." This band was so polished right out of the gate and I was just hypnotized by the lead singer Stephen Pearcy's unique voice.

I got a call from a friend in the neighborhood who asked if I wanted to go see Ratt at the Sporto. Of course I agreed. That night he showed up at my house to drive me there in one of those Volkswagen Bugs that looked like the car in the *Herbie* movies. I jumped in the car and we took off towards the

Sporto. During that ride my friend reveals to me that he had Thai stick with him to smoke. I had only been smoking pot for a few years by then and I never even seen Thai stick in person. It was mostly a 1970s thing and by 1983 it had almost disappeared from the drug scene altogether. I heard about it, but for me it was like folklore or something because I was never exposed to it or had seen it anywhere. We got to the parking lot of the Sporto and he pulled it out once we were parked. My friend handed it to me and it really did look like a stick. There were no seeds like marijuana and all we had to do was pull these leaves off the stick and roll them up in some paper. I sat there and rolled us up a joint, which I was very good at by the way, and lit it up.

We sat there in his VW Bug and puffed away. I was so tired, because I did not get much sleep the night before and I was hoping this would wake me up or give me some energy. The buzz hit me like a hurricane and fast. Everything started to get cloudy with my vision. I felt like it was the double vision Foreigner sang about. We both got out of the car and started walking around in the parking lot completely baked from the smoke.

On one side of the building there was this huge tour bus and we walked right up to it. Sitting in a folding lawn chair at the entrance of the bus was this long-haired, old, hippie dude that welcomed us and told us to come aboard. Without any fear, like young people, we just walked into this strange bus. My buddy came in behind me and as soon as we focused our eyes on the people there, we realized it was the band Ratt. I almost shit my pants! I could not believe we were in their tour bus! As we walked towards the back of the bus there was the lead singer, Stephen Pearcy, with his back towards us and his pants down. There was a woman on her knees that we could not get a good look at, but we could tell that she was blowing him. Robbin Crosby, the guitarist, was sitting down on the couch smoking a joint and he waved us over. I sat next to him as he strummed a riff from the song *Wanted Man* and passed the joint to me. I could not believe we were hanging out with Ratt; my head nearly exploded from excitement!

Just when Stephen started to moan and climax, the hippie guy stepped onto the bus and yelled, "Twenty minutes to curtain!" He motioned for me and my friend to leave, so I turned and got one last look at the band for posterity as we got off the bus. The two of us were looking each other straight in the eyes saying, "Holy shit that was cool!"

As we walked away, we passed this old school bus that looked like it was a leftover from the sixty's revolution or something. Some guy was standing in the doorway and said that he saw what bus we were just on. As we walked up to him to tell how cool that was, he went into the old school bus throwing us a slight wave, so we followed him inside. As soon as we walked onto the bus, I knew something felt wrong. The entire bus was gutted out. Where the seats used to be were nothing but milk crates lining both sides of the bus with candles burning on them. The guy walked towards the back and sat down on a crate covered with a tiger-skin rug.

As we walked towards the back of the bus to tell this old hippie our Ratt story, the guy screamed,

"Did you see the rats?" He pulled out what looked like the bloody body of a dead rat and a huge Norman Bates butcher knife. Immediately, we both screamed and ran towards the entrance of the bus while the guy ran towards us with the bloody rat and knife in his hand. I felt like I was stuck in the movie *The Shining* where I was running down this endless hallway. Everything slowed down and it felt like I was running forever. I could hear the guy's footsteps getting closer and gaining on me. I felt a gust of wind fly by my right ear and I then saw the body of the bloody rat flying by. The dead body of the rat passed me and slammed into the windshield in front of me with a horrible *splat*. The image of the rat spread eagle with all four legs spread out across the windshield eerily glowed red in the candlelight. My friend made it out of the bus first and as I hit the steps I slipped and fell. I smashed my head on the door and immediately passed out cold.

I don't know how much time passed, but I woke up with my buddy shaking me. As my eyes came into focus I saw him trying to revive me and telling me to come on, that we've got to go, the concert is about to start. I looked around and I realized I was back in the Volkswagen Bug with my buddy. I asked him about the guy with the knife and my friend started looking at me like I was insane.

I said, "What about the band? We met the band, Ratt!"

My friend just looked at me and said, "Man, you passed out stoned! We have not left the car, there is no guy with a knife and we damn sure have not met the group Ratt!"

I stepped out of the car realizing it was all a dream. I just walked, slightly perplexed, towards the Sporto's entrance. It wasn't too long before I realized what a freaking wonderful stick this really was and how it hit me. It was like pot, but way stronger. Not for nothing, but I will never forget Thai stick and I will never forget meeting the band Ratt, even if it was a dream.

We made our way inside the Sporto still blazed on Thai stick and took in the crowd, the vibe and of course Ratt. Either that drug made me think Ratt was unbelievable or they really were on fire that night. I can say, when I think of 1983, I remember Thai stick and the great show Ratt put on that year. It was not the last time I would see the band Ratt play live, but it was the last and only time I ever saw, smoked or enjoyed Thai stick ever again. All I can say is that it was a wonderful drug and that memory at the Sporto that night was an enjoyable one for me.

Chapter Six: 1984

The year 1984 was an amazing year in music, but I must say just thinking about it makes me feel old. That was over thirty years ago. It was a time and place that seemed like another world looking back at it. Movie tickets cost $2.50 to get in the theater. A gallon of milk cost $1.10 and the average cost of a new home in America was $86,730. Hell, the median income in America at the time was $21,600 and the average rent was only $350 a month. Even Ticket Master Tickets to a concert were less than twenty dollars. Sadly we had more buying power back then and our dollar went way further than it does today.

Rolling Stone magazine declared 1984 as Pop's greatest year but Pop Music was not my thing. For me it was a great year of music for completely different reasons. Prince, Michael Jackson and

Madonna had nothing on a new band called Bon Jovi that debuted their first album that year as far as I was concerned. Their mash hit "Runaway" was way better than any of that Pop crap that was being force fed to us by the corporations that were slowly taking over the music industry.

In my world, 1984 started off with the band Yes having the number one song in the country called "Owner of a Lonely Heart" and the year ended with Def Leppard's drummer losing his arm in a car crash. What made the year unforgettable for me and music history was what happened between the beginning and the end of that year in music. As far as the Sporto went, many bands in my world came through South Florida that year like the Scorpions, Rush and Aerosmith. Judas Priest, Motely Crüe and Yes certainly made their mark in our music temple that year, but no one and I mean no one had a year like Van Halen. People forget when Michael Jackson's *Thriller* album sat at number one in America, right below it at number two was Van Halen's album *1984*. How anyone can talk about that year without acknowledging Van Halen and their rocketing to the biggest band in the world status is beyond me. Van Halen exploded that year and became bigger than they ever were before. Songs like "Jump," "Panama" and "Hot for Teacher" consumed the airways. You could not turn on the radio for more than 10 minutes without hearing Van Halen that year. None of us knew at the time this was going to be the last album with David Lee Roth. When I went to see them at the Hollywood Sportatorium on their *1984* Tour, I had no idea that was the end of a historic musical era. All I knew was that it was the best concert I'd seen at the Sporto that year and nothing was close. Van Halen was in a groove despite their inner turmoil. They never played so well. By 1984, Eddie Van Halen was considered by everyone with a set of ears the best guitarist in the world. Even the Jackson Family had Eddie fly out to Dallas, Texas to appear as a special guest just to play a live guitar solo of the Michael Jackson's song called "Beat It". David Lee Roth was giving every front man in the world a class study on fronting a band. Van Halen even had the best MTV Videos that year with "Hot for Teacher", "Panama" and the song "I'll Wait" on constant rotation. Van Halen was on top of the world and here is what I remember.

My buddy Chuck, who I grew up with was a huge Van Halen fan and we decided to take our girlfriends to see them live. The girls were big fans of Van Halen, but they were there to see the opening band Autograph, too. At the time, Autograph was new on the scene and they had a huge hit called "Turn Up the Radio." The ladies wanted to see them badly. We got our tickets the usual way and made it to the Sporto on the night of January 20, 1984. We smoked our share of weed that night, but what my friends did not know was that I took a Quaalude before the concert. In the mid-80s one of the most popular drugs in America was a pill called Quaalude. The version of that pill that took off in South Florida was called Lemmon 7-14. Quaaludes were everywhere back then and some guy from the neighborhood gave me one and I saved it for the Van Halen concert. For those of you not familiar with this pill, when you take it, the pill makes you feel drunk without having to drink. That is the best way I can describe a

Lemmon 7-14. It was a drunk feeling that was very intense and it felt wild because you did not need to have a drink to feel that way but only take a pill. Stupid me at the time decided to drink on top of taking that pill and that did not actually work out for me. I was in this strange state of mind. I did not realize what I was doing at the time. I was in some strange head space, but when I found out many years later my behavior, I was horrified. In the drug scene in South Florida in the 1980s different drugs came and went. Some were good experiences. Some were not. That drug turned me into someone I did not recognize. I was so singularly focused on the stage during the concert that I did not even realize what I was doing. I just remember what an amazing show Van Halen put on and how David Lee Roth was running all around the stage doing his signature jumps. We had great seats and I stood there mesmerized by Eddie Van Halen's guitar solo. Despite my abhorrent behavior that I'm too ashamed to mention but apologize for vehemently, the concert stood out for me as the best of 1984 in the Sporto that year.

Chapter Seven: 1985

The year 1985 was a strange year for my kind of music. There really was not a whole lot going on in the Hard Rock scene. The year was consumed by big musical events like *Live Aid* and *Farm Aid*. MTV launched a new channel called VH1 and everyone was going around singing, "We Are the World." As far as the Hard Rock genre that year, Foreigner was busy destroying their band with the pussified song "I want to Know What Love Is" and Judas Priest had two fans shoot themselves. They claimed playing Judas Priest songs backwards creates voices that tell them to kill. One of the two teens that shot themselves died. It really was a strange year for Hard Rock. A bunch of parents formed a group called *P.M.R.C.* or *The Parents Music Resource Center* and had a hearing in front of The U.S. Senate about censorship and rock music. Dee Snider of Twisted

Sister even found himself testifying in front of our nation's politicians.

There were some good things in my world of music that year. After being fired from Metallica, Dave Mustaine started a band called Megadeth and released their first album. Heart released the only album of theirs to go number one with the single "These Dreams." The Scorpions released a live album and AC/DC released an Album called *Fly on the Wall* in an attempt to return to their earlier raw sound. The album was almost like a protest to the Glam Metal scene. I forgave them for that insult to my kind of music. Every band makes a misstep at one time or another and that band had been through a lot. Dokken and my favorite band Triumph released new albums in 1985 while KISS released the album *Asylum*. Bon Jovi and Ratt were still kicking ass respectively with a couple of new albums and the Hard Rock scene was trucking along.

By 1985 the crack epidemic was in full bloom in South Florida. Entire neighborhoods were being consumed by this drug and its arrival on the drug scene made a huge impact. It must be said that not everyone who followed the Hard Rock scene did drugs. Most did not or just smoked a little weed. However, I did drugs and for me it would be hard to draft a book about the 1980s, the Hard Rock scene and South Florida without mentioning the drugs that came and went in that era. When it came to my drug use, I was mostly just a pothead and a drinker, but I wanted to have an opinion on drugs, so I would try most anything at least once. Strangely for me I actually tried smoking cocaine before I ever tried snorting it. Crack, as it was called, was a form of cocaine that was cooked up so you could smoke it. It was everywhere in 1985 and I did enough of it to kill an elephant twice over. That September I smoked just enough crack to lose my senses and land up at a Bruce Springsteen Concert. This was the year that The Boss exploded on the music scene with the album *Born in the U.S.A.* and had a huge tour. The album, the man and his music were against everything that I believed in. It represented the epitomic selling out of commercial or corporate greed and the whole thing made me sick. It was hard to go anywhere that year without hearing that drivel from that album on the radio and MTV. Somehow I landed up at the Orange Bowl Stadium in Miami on September 9, 1985 watching Bruce Springsteen and the E Street Band play for four hours. I must have been on crack that year if I landed up at that concert. If that is not a reason not to do drugs, then I don't know what is. They should run public service announcements on TV stating, "If you smoke crack you could land up at a Springsteen concert." They could show a teenager strapped to a chair like in the movie *Clockwork Orange* with his eyelids taped opened, as the kid watches Bruce over and over again singing "Born in the U.S.A.," and that would have ended the crack epidemic.

Despite Bruce Springsteen, *Live Aid* and *Farm Aid* that year the Hollywood Sportatorium still provided us with some great Hard Rock bands to see live. Some very good bands came through that year like Iron Maiden, Twisted Sister, Rush and Motley Crüe. That year Broward County was finally widening the road out to the Sporto to a four-lane deal. For some reason they only widened Pines Boulevard from

University Drive to Flamingo Road and left the last four miles a two-lane bottleneck situation leading up to the arena. Maybe the people who designed those plans were caught up in the crack epidemic as well, now that I think about it. That was a ridiculous decision that caused even more road rage. That year Triumph came through and I missed them due to some family issues. They were my favorite band and I never got over missing their concert in January of 1985. However other bands came through like AC/DC who brought with them a new badass guitarist on the scene to open their concert by the name of Yngwie Malmsteen. Yngwie was an incredible guitarist who would give Eddie Van Halen a run for his money as the best guitarist in the world.

Looking back on 1985 I must say the best concert that year was Ratt and Bon Jovi. Ratt was on their *Invasion of Your Privacy* Tour and Bon Jovi was on their *7800 Fahrenheit* Tour. Both bands were in their prime and no one knew who the hell Bon Jovi was yet. Bon Jovi actually out-shined Ratt as the opening band, even though Ratt kicked ass. I remember the lights going off in the Sporto and then all of a sudden a spotlight lights up on Jon Bon Jovi who somehow was now standing on a platform at the back of the arena. It was wild, because he was on stage when the lights went out and in no time flat there he was in the back. The whole arena turned their heads towards him shining in the spotlight while he sang "Runaway" with a guitar strapped around his shoulder.

For those of you reading this right now, I have no words in the English Dictionary to describe how good he sang that song. We were so lucky to have seen and heard him in his prime vocally. I mean the man could never hit that high note at the end of the song "Runaway" nowadays, but in 1985 he nailed it live right in front me. It was an incredible experience that brought a tear to my eyes. I cannot stand Jon Bon Jovi now, all these years later, after he sold out and left us all, but I knew and saw the band Bon Jovi before anyone ever heard of them. I am telling you, "That fucking band could rock!" At the end of his set Jon Bon Jovi grabbed the mic and told the crowd, "The next time you see us we will not be an opening band; we will be headlining." Man oh man was he right. We did not know then what he knew when he told us that. It was the last Bon Jovi Tour before they exploded on the world with the album *Slippery When Wet*. We were a part of music history and I was there. I will never forget that concert. Ratt and Bon Jovi was the best show at the Sporto in 1985, in my humble opinion.

Chapter Eight: 1986

The year 1986 started off with the first inductions to the Rock and Roll Hall of Fame and the decision to build the actual building in Cleveland, Ohio. It was also the year that the official War on Drugs started when the federal government enacted the Anti-Drug Abuse Act of 1986 and changed our prison system from rehabilitative to punitive. The bill brought forth mandatory minimum sentencing guidelines for drugs including marijuana, while giving birth to the most racist sentencing disparities ever seen between crack and powder cocaine.

Meanwhile the world of Hard Rock was kicking ass. So many bands made it through the Sporto that year. For me this was the year that I went to see my favorite band of all times, Triumph. Because of my obvious bias with Triumph, I would no doubt pick that as the best concert of that year for The

Hollywood Sportatorium. Since I cannot be objective with this subject, I will talk about some other concerts that I saw that year that were also amazing before I get into the Triumph Concert and its utter brilliance.

It is hard to understate how big 1986 was in the world of music when one looks at what happened to Van Halen. After the success of their album *1984*, the band and David Lee Roth parted ways. Sammy Hagar was chosen to replace Roth as the front man and lead singer. It was an earthquake in the world of Hard Rock. All of us loved Sammy and his solo career. He was called the Red Rocker and the man earned everyone's respect with his music. We just did not know how this would pan out with Van Halen. It was the talk of the town for a while and a huge debate amongst head bangers. All of the back and forth between us Hard Rockers ended with the release of Van Halen's first album with Sammy Hagar called *5150*. That album put to rest forever whether or not Van Halen could move forward. To date, it was the best album they ever made with Sammy, in my opinion, even though future albums would sail into the stratosphere. Sammy Hagar brought Van Halen from playing arenas to playing in front of packed stadiums. That album peaked at number one and surpassed their last album *1984* which only made it to number two on the Billboard Charts. The name *5150* was the name of Eddie Van Halen's studio in California and the term *5150* was a California law enforcement term that meant there was a mentally disturbed person. The Red Rocker took the band to another level but before all of that happened they came to play the Hollywood Sportatorium and rocked South Florida on April 7th, 1986.

I have to admit the 5150 Tour was a hell of a show to see. I remember my girlfriend of the time sitting on the steps of the Sporto throwing up as I kept begging her to get her act together. The band was just about to start and here she was being a lightweight with her drinking and ruining the chance for me to see music history. As soon as I heard the show start with Sammy's guitar riff and him singing the Kinks cover that Van Halen did called "You Really Got Me," I took off running. I left my drunken girlfriend behind swimming in her own vomit and sprinted towards the arena and my seat. Like a schmuck, I just left her there with her girlfriend on the front steps and made my way to music history. Our relationship clearly did not last the test of time, but my love for Van Halen sure the fuck did. The show was incredible. Sammy did not feel comfortable singing most Van Halen songs that David sang, so they mostly just played the album *5150* and did a Led Zeppelin cover of the song "Rock and Roll" as an encore. There was a platform that was built above our heads and Sammy ran around up there singing "I Can't Drive 55" and playing his guitar. People forget Sammy Hagar was and is no joke when it comes to playing guitar. It was just a great concert.

Another great concert at the Sporto that year was Judas Priest and Dokken on June 18th, 1986. That year a short documentary was made and released called *Heavy Metal Parking Lot* that covered the tailgating outside of an arena on this tour. If you ever get a chance to see that film, look it up. The film shows the Hard Rock scene at the time and the people who made it. It is a beautiful look back in time and space and truly captures the spirit of this book. The concert itself was fantastic and Dokken never played better. Judas Priest was on top of the world and in the peak of their success. I had a great night on powder cocaine and Heavy Metal. It was the time in my life that I went from smoking crack to just doing powder. It is amazing to look back at the fact that my gateway drug to powder cocaine, was actually crack. That is an amazing factoid and a true sign of that time.

It is impossible to talk about the Heavy Metal or Hard Rock scene in the 1980s without mentioning Ozzy Osbourne. From Black Sabbath to the work he did with Randy Rhodes, Ozzy was intertwined with our music like oxygen is intertwined with life. There is no life without oxygen and there is no Heavy Metal or Hard Rock without Ozzy Osbourne. I finally got to see Ozzy on September 5, 1986, with Queensrÿche opening up for him. Ozzy was a Metal god and Queensrÿche was loved by all of us because their lead singer Geoff Tate was the first opera singer to go Heavy Metal.

I made it to the Sporto that night on time despite the traffic issues and was able to catch the whole show. Queensrÿche blew my mind away because they sounded exactly like their studio stuff live. Geoff's voice was one of the most crystal clear and beautiful voices I had ever heard live. The band was spot on and really outshined Ozzy that night. That year, Ozzy was in his bloated stage and they lowered him down on this giant seat from the roof of the Sporto to the stage. He was so fat at the time I thought the cables would break. His voice was still vintage Ozzy, but it was the only time I saw this Hard Rock god and I do feel a little gypped that I never got to see Ozzy in his prime. However, the show was still worth seeing and I do get to claim I did see Ozzy live in concert.

In the ongoing saga that year with Van Halen and David Lee Roth, David released his competing album to *5150* entitled *Eat 'Em and Smile*. Roth put together what became known as The David Lee Roth Band which was a revolving door of rock superstars. They had a lot of commercial success and came through the Sporto with a band opening for them that I wanted to see bad called Cinderella. The band just released their debut album *Night Songs* in August and it exploded onto the scene and raced up the charts eventually making it to number three on Billboard.

On November 14th, 1986, I made my way to the Sporto to see this tour. Roth was all over the radio and MTV at the time with songs like "Yankee Rose," "Tobacco Road" and "That's Life." Cinderella was in their prime shooting to the top of their fame, so this tour was the talk of the town. Everyone wanted to get a ticket and the ladies went crazy trying to get to this show. It was the hottest ticket in a long time. From the moment Cinderella sang "Night Songs" and "Nobody's Fool" to the end of the show with Dave singing his encore "California Girls," the Sporto stood in awe. The fact that David sang my favorite Van Halen song "On Fire" would have made this concert the best show to have seen that year, if not for Triumph. It is hard to believe nowadays, after David Lee Roth devolved into the sad cartoon he seems today, but David was really good back in the day. Cinderella made me a lifelong fan and guaranteed that night I would see them again. However, as I said earlier, this was the year I went to see my favorite band Triumph.

When I got wind that Triumph was coming to the Hollywood Sportatorium, I lost my mind. I had already missed them once and was not going to let that happen again. This time I was hell-bent on getting great seats for the concert. I wanted to get on the floor of the Sporto right in front of that stage. I wanted, I needed, I had to get the best tickets I ever had for any concert in the Sporto, period. Because I did not have a credit card at that age, the only way to get the seats I was going for was to camp out overnight at the mall. I needed to be one of the first people in line when the Hollywood Mall opened their doors at 10 a.m. and let the public go in to shop.

My friend Chuck and I got to the mall the night before and were one of the first few people in line on the sidewalk outside of the closest entrance to the music store that sold the tickets. As the night progressed, the sidewalk filled with people showing up with tents, blankets and pillows to make it through the night. Chuck and I never thought of any of that. We had to sit right on the cement sidewalk and tough it out. It was a great night. It was the first and only time in the history of my life I sat out in front of a store and camped out overnight to buy something. For me, this wasn't just something to buy. This was my ticket to music heaven. I had spent countless nights in my bedroom wearing out Triumph albums and cassettes. Now I was finally going to have the band sing it all for me live. It was a great time to be a Hard Rock fan. We had a memorable night camping out on the sidewalk under the stars. We smoked weed all night and told stories of the Hollywood Sportatorium with the rest of the head bangers on the sidewalk. Everyone there had their Sporto story to tell and had their favorite band. We argued over rock bands, rock music and live concerts. We stayed up all night with fellow-minded Hard Rock enthusiasts and did a little bit of cocaine to make it through the night. A cop car pulled up to all of us and rolled his window down. He asked us who was playing this time. We yelled out, "Triumph," but the police officer looked like he had never heard of the band. Then someone on the sidewalk yelled out, "Bad Company is opening!" and the cop's face changed revealing he knew that band. As he drove away we could hear the cop singing "All Right Now" as he rolled the window back up.

The morning came as we watched all of the mall workers go into the side doors of the mall for work that day. Two hours later the mall doors opened up and we all sprinted towards the music store completely abandoning any sense of fairness of who was in line or where in line they were all night. It must have looked like the Running of the Bulls to passersby. When all the line settled in front of the register and the cash had been exchanged, I looked down in my hands and saw brand new Triumph tickets for row seven right in front of the stage. I could not believe it. Despite the fact that Ticketmaster was already selling tickets over the phone to people with credit cards since 8 a.m. I still landed up with the best seats I had ever had for any concert at the Sporto ever. It was like the rock gods understood what this all meant to me and they aligned all of the stars in the universe to make it happen.

Triumph, for those of you folks who don't know, was a Canadian Hard Rock band which was a trio like Rush. Their lead singer and guitarist was Ric Emmitt. Gil Moore was their drummer and other lead singer and Mike Levine was the bassist. These three guys together created some of the greatest music that ever came out of Canada. It was one of those situations that without each other, they could never reach perfection, but when the three were and are together something special happens that is unforgettable. They align like Orion's Belt in the sky and together make their mark on the universe. They were like a three-legged stool that only stood when all three legs were there. Triumph's musicians were serious rock 'n' rollers and held a master class live on stage for the world to see when it came to playing their instruments. These guys were the masters, the teachers and they were *my* rock gods. I think as a writer, what has always drawn me to this band was their lyrics. These guys were modern day poets. They had things to say and they said them better than anyone back in the day. They sang and wrote populists songs for the masses, for the common man, while backing up their lyrics with such clear skills on their instruments. It is unbelievable that only three guys made that beautiful sound.

By the time I got to see them in 1986 I had no idea the band was just less than two years away from breaking up. They were touring on the *Sport of Kings* album which was a clear shift towards a more palatable sound for the radio. *Sport of Kings* was an album made with the direct intention to cash in commercially. For some reason, reaching for the very top of the Billboard charts or filling their bank accounts became more important than the music. That might be unfair to say, but that is what it looked like to a lot of people. Don't get me wrong, *Sport of Kings* produced some good songs like "Tears in the Rain" and "Somebody's Out There," but the band was clearly making the same mistake that KISS made with the song "I Was made For Lovin' You." I don't blame them. It didn't make me angry. I loved whatever they did. I was their fan and I would stay with them and follow them down any musical direction. I loved the harder and bluesy stuff earlier in their career, but if these guys needed to make some money and put a nest egg aside for themselves by going more commercial, then who was I to judge? All I know is that these three guys produced the best music I have ever heard and on December 6, 1986, I walked into the Hollywood Sportatorium and took my seat in the seventh row right in front of the stage.

The opening band that night was Bad Company. It was the year 1986 that Bad Company replaced their lead singer and gave Brian Howe the reigns. The former lead singer Paul Rodgers went on to form a super group called The Firm and for me Brian was the perfect replacement for Bad Company. Most people sided with Paul Rodgers and his version of Bad Company, but that was easy to predict. People voted with their hearts most of the time, but it must be said that the Brian Howe era was kick ass and was just fine for my taste. Bad Company sounded excellent that night.

I had such a good seat I was afraid to leave for even a bathroom break in fear of losing my spot.

After the opening band the lights went back on and I stood there just waiting for my boys to appear. Suddenly, after a time, the lights went dark and the curtain once again was lifted, but this time Triumph had the stage. The first thing I realized was that the lights that always appeared spelling out Triumph behind the band were way brighter in person than watching it on MTV. I could feel the heat of the bulbs when the band's name would light up behind the drum set. The band opened up with their classic "Fight the Good Fight" hit and I was screaming and going nuts. I was so close. I felt like they could look into my eyes. I was like some schoolhouse bitch waiting on the tarmac for the Beatles to get off the plane, but fuck the Beatles. They sucked. This was Triumph. I melted into the stew of a groupie, real fan and teenaged angst all in one. I must have screamed throughout the entire first song, because the next thing I knew the band transitioned into the next song off their latest album "Tears in The Rain." I was just learning this new album *Sport of Kings* and hearing this new song live almost made my head explode. The band played the songs "Spellbound" and "Somebody's Out There" and I just knew at that moment this was the best band in the history of music. My proof came when they played "Magic Power" and "Lay It on The Line" with such perfection. By the time they played "Follow Your Heart" and their guitar and drum solos, I knew without a shadow of a doubt, the Canadian band Triumph had no peers. They were the best Hard Rock band in the world, period. December 6, 1986, was the one and only time I ever got to see Triumph play live. A couple of years after that night in 1988 Ric Emmett left the band and they broke up forever from its original form. Phil X replaced Ric on the band's tenth album *Edge of Excess*. They had some live album released, post break up, including one reunited show in Sweden, but for us fans, there would be no Triumph reunion. On March 10, 2007, Triumph was finally inducted into the Canadian Music Industry's Hall of Fame in a ceremony at the Toronto's Fairmont Royal York Hotel. All three original members of the band showed up for that well deserved event. I believe it is now time for the Rock 'n' Roll Hall of Fame in Ohio to welcome these three master musicians into their ranks. It has been a long time coming. All I have left is all the music they created, my memories of seeing them play live and their images on my computer for my desktop to my screensaver. It will remain there until I die. I carry their music with me still. I will always be a Triumph fan. I'm an old man now going on fifty years old as I write this and I have played their music to my daughter her whole life. She is ten now and I convey to her a timeless message from Triumph. I tell her to listen to her heart and "Hold On" to her dreams.

Chapter Nine: 1987

The Hard Rock era was in full flux by 1987 and doing just fine. The L.A. scene produced yet another new band that year called Guns 'n Roses. A UK band called Whitesnake broke through and showed how the Glam Metal Scene traveled and influenced people around the world. Even the band The Cult released their third album that year and shifted to more of a Heavy Metal sound. Motley Crüe released their fourth album *Girls, Girls, Girls* and that shot up to number two on the U.S. charts. The band Faster Pussycat debuted their first album and became another well-known band out of Los Angeles and the Glam Metal scene. Everything in our world was trucking along just fine. You could not turn on the radio in 1987 without hearing my kind of music all over the place. Def Leppard released their number one album by the name *Hysteria* and landed four top ten hits that year. Our music took front seat for all the world to see and hear. It felt like it would last forever. The music was incredible. I even broke away from the Sporto a couple of times that year and went to go see Ace Frehley with his new band called Frehley's Comets down in Miami in a tiny venue called the Cameo Theater. The place only held around three thousand people so it was an amazing place to see a concert. White Lion opened up for them and the whole night became an unforgettable experience. That year the drug of choice was hash and hash oil and there was no better place to indulge in that than the Pink Floyd Concert in the middle of a thunderstorm at the Orange Bowl in Miami on November 1, 1987. Nowadays they would have cancelled that show due to lightning. We were not as pussified as a nation back then. The show must go on. That is how we were raised.

The Sporto that year saw their share of my bands. Def Leppard with Tesla played the Sportatorium while Motley Crüe came with their opening band by the name of Guns 'n Roses. Ratt,

Poison and Iron Maiden made their mark on our stage once again and put on memorable shows. However, nothing that year topped Bon Jovi's triumphant return to the Sporto as the headliner bringing Ratt with them as their opening band. That was the show of the year. On February 14, 1987, I walked into the Sporto to see Bon Jovi play once again. That day they had the number one song in the nation "Livin' on a Prayer," which became the biggest song of that year in the entire world. That is a hell of a claim to make, but that night we all walked into the Sporto, Bon Jovi was on top of the world and nobody was bigger. To see their first tour as a headliner *Slippery When Wet* and watching this band that I knew before anyone else knew, was an incredible treat for me. I knew this was a special band when I first saw them and when they became the biggest band in the world that year, I felt vindicated about my taste in music. I had a good ear for talent and this proved it. They put on a great show and Ratt completely kicked ass that night. Looking back at it, it seems eerie now, knowing my genre of music was about to be decimated in the

1990s by what was called The Seattle Sound or Grunge Music. Even our favorite arena, the Sporto, was about to be demolished forever. We had no clue what was ahead. There was a storm on the horizon for head bangers everywhere, but in the year 1987 we had no idea. We were on top of the world. The entire music world bowed down at the knees of our Glam Metal gods. It was our Hard Rock Bands and their music that ruled the entire universe. It was a movement that seemed unstoppable.

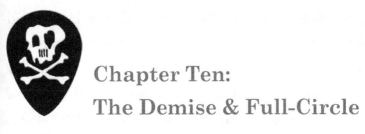

Chapter Ten:
The Demise & Full-Circle

The 1980s were winding down and the 1990s were about to smash the only world I ever knew into a million pieces. In October of 1988 a group and a music sound started to bubble up out of Seattle. A band called Soundgarden released their debut album. It was a new style of music called Grunge. By the beginning of the 1990s, the Seattle Sound, as it is now called, exploded onto the music scene with a band called Nirvana and changed music forever. At the very same time, South Florida built a state of the art brand new venue called the Miami Arena. This arena changed the live concert scene permanently in South Florida. The acts that came to the Sportatorium hated playing there. A brand-new arena in Miami was what they desired for many years. Well, the musical acts got their state-of-the-art arena to play in, but the fans lost their Hard Rock milieu and home. The last Hard Rock show in the Hollywood Sportatorium was Judas Priest with Cinderella opening for them on September 18, 1988. Ironically the Sporto was known as the heavy-metal mecca of South Florida, but their final show on October 21, 1988 was the country music acts Highway 101, The Desert Rose Band, and Larry Boone.

According to *Wikipedia*: *In 1991, a franchise owner in the newly formed Continental Hockey Association proposed spending $6 million to renovate the Sportatorium and negotiated a buy/lease agreement with Stephen Calder's heirs. The new team was to be called the Florida Makos, but shortly before the owner was due to put down a deposit on the Sportatorium and commence renovations, the fledgling hockey league failed. A month later, a developer proposed building 1,500 homes on the site and surrounding land, and the Pembroke Pines City Commission voted to change the land's zoning from commercial recreation to residential. In 1992, the Broward County Planning Council approved plans for 1,260 homes and a small shopping center on the site. In 1993, after several years of disuse as well as* *hurricane damage from the previous year's Hurricane Andrew, the Hollywood Sportatorium was torn down.*

Last, but not least, even the drug scene changed when a drug called Ecstasy made its way from Europe to our shores in the late 80s, early 90s. The world of just doing some weed, coke or opium was changed insidiously with the designer drug called Ecstasy. This drug created a Frankenstein version of all of them combined. No longer were people doing drugs given to us by Mother Nature from the cannabis and poppy plant. Now people were creating designer pills in the laboratory that made the drug scene more wicked and pernicious. Parties called Raves took hold in America and swept across the nation. Ecstasy, Rave parties and electronic dance music out of Detroit, Michigan called Techno stood in place of Hard Rock shows. Everything seemed to have changed on a dime. My world, our world, the Hard Rock world of the 80s was gone in the blink of an eye. All that is left is the memories of sex, drugs and rock 'n' roll. It was an incredible time to be alive. It was an amazing time to come of age. I feel so fortunate and special that I was there and a part of it all. It was so much fun.

I'm an old man now going towards fifty years old, like I said before, and I asked myself, "What was the best way to end this book?" After much thought on that subject, I decided to end it where it all started for me. I called up my mother who is going on seventy years of age and I asked her if she remembered that she took me to my first concert when I was eleven years old to see Fleetwood Mac. She said, "Of Course I do." I said, "Mom I want to take my ten-year-old daughter and you to see Fleetwood Mac on March 23, 2015, at the Amway Center in Orlando, Florida." My mom screamed, "Absolutely!" and started to cry. I sat my ten-year-old daughter down and explained to her that I was going to take her to her first live concert with grandma. She screamed, "Taylor Swift!" and I said, "No baby, Fleetwood Mac." and her face just looked confused. I sat her down on my lap in front of my computer and pulled up YouTube and started to play Fleetwood Mac songs. As soon as she heard Stevie Nick's voice she got very excited saying, "We are going to see her sing?" I said, "She is only one singer in that band, baby, and we are going to see the whole band play." I explained to her that the stars in the sky just aligned and that "Christy McVie just returned to the band after such a long absence and that Fleetwood Mac was whole again just for you, me and grandma." I played songs all night from all of the different singers and albums of Fleetwood Mac. She went to school the next day telling all her friends she was going to a concert. I doubt if anyone but her teacher knew who Fleetwood Mac was in that 4th grade class, but my kid was proud and lit up like a Christmas tree.

So on March 23, 2015, I loaded up the minivan with my mother and my daughter and headed toward the city of Orlando. It was full circle for me. Taking three generations of my family to this concert was very emotional. Authoring this book was extremely emotional for me, when all the memories came flooding back. Music affects me very deeply. I never had that experience with my other books. With my hands on the wheel, I drove towards what felt like destiny. I drove towards the city of Orlando.

I had to go find the Amway Center. I had never been there before.

The three of us arrived in downtown Orlando and found event parking in this downtown garage that was three blocks from the Amway center. Because the arena is downtown, there is very little parking close or near the building that was not a laborious walking distance. We entered the building and found our seats. The Amway Center is kind of like an Opera House the way it is set up inside. The seats and levels are built upward in a circle. This is the place that the NBA team the Orlando Heat play. The Hollywood Sportatorium had a capacity just under the Amway Center, which holds twenty thousand people.

I have seen countless concerts in my life in many different places since the Sporto closed, from California to Florida. However, I had never seen a concert in such an uncomfortable arena. As far as the Amway Center as a venue, I hated it. It was like being on a plane with no legroom and having that feeling that you are being crushed like sardines in a can. When I sat down, up on the balcony, my knees were already on the back of the head of the person sitting in front of me. It was beyond horrible. If it wasn't for the nature of why I was there and who I was with, I would have just left under any other circumstance. I will never return there again for any event whatsoever, well, maybe a Triumph reunion. Whoever designed that place only cared about cramming as many people in it as possible and cared nothing about people's comfort. He should be hung on the sidewalk in front of the place by the authorities as a warning to the next greedy bastard whose apathy of the public creates this situation. It was quite a shame because this is a newer building. The tickets were one hundred dollars apiece so I felt extremely angry over the whole ordeal.

Luckily, my anger abated as soon as the lights went down and Fleetwood Mac hit the stage. I watched my daughter light up like a Christmas tree as soon as she heard the live music. The band was incredible. Fleetwood Mac's set list covered decades of their music. They interacted with the crowd and told stories about the band and how certain songs came about. It literally was magical. Unlike the Sporto the acoustics were amazing inside. The band really got a shot in the arm with the return of their songbird Christy McVie. They were thrilled she was back and the band was whole again. Stevie Nicks told a story about a song she wrote when she was fifteen years old and how the band started in San Francisco. Lindsey Buckingham talked about the ups and downs of the band over the years. It was so special to be a part of this tour and see them play in 2015. I realized it was thirty-five years since the Tusk Tour when my mother and I had seen Fleetwood Mac play. Thirty-five years and they still sounded awesome. I looked over at my mom during the show and I saw her crying. I looked down at my daughter and watched her filled with joy clapping along with the crowd. It really was a special night. I send out my unending gratitude to Fleetwood Mac and thank them for all of the music and memories Of course they are not my Hard Rock crowd, but they can play their instruments just as hard as the next band when they let loose. I feel like they are part of my family now and played such a huge role in my love for live music.

In the end, those of us from South Florida that were part of the Hard Rock scene at The Hollywood Sportatorium in the 1980s moved away and scattered to the wind. However, we are bound together from the four corners of the Earth and will forever be connected to each other through our experiences and the music we all heard at the Sporto. I never changed my taste in music although I expanded it, and I am sure that is the same for most of you. For now, just email me your Sporto stories and if I get enough of them, I might publish a book filled with your truths and your experiences there. Give me suggestions for a title and maybe we can do something special collectively. In the meanwhile, I love you all and will leave with you the words from the best damn group there ever was, Triumph...

Music holds the secret.
To know it can make you whole.
It's not just a game of notes,
it's the sound inside your soul.
The magic of the melody
runs through you like a stream.
The notes they play
flow through your head
    Like a dream,
        Like a dream,
            Like a dream.

TRIUMPH

About The Author

C. Rich is an author, poet, freelance ghostwriter and blogger. He grew up on the streets and beaches of South Florida and has a "baked in" perspective of life. He is a consumer of all things American culture and gives his opinion on all of it.

He is a lifelong backpacker and has climbed the highest mountains east of the Mississippi that the country has to offer. He has also climbed a large portion of the Appalachian Trail from Springer Mountain in Georgia to Mt. Katahdin in Maine. His writings have been recognized by CNBC and his words have reached across the globe.

Love him or hate him, because there is nothing in between. He has been called the Archie Bunker of the Twenty-First Century and he rails against political correctness. C. Rich sees the world through a sarcastic and sardonic mind. Following his writing is a journey of political incorrectness, discovery and pure madness.

Made in the USA
Monee, IL
12 July 2025